Detail from the top of a box, raised work on white satin: Bathsheba bathing, attended by her maid. The trellis archway has flowers and fruit in detached lace stitch. The attendant wears an embroidered dress, lace-stitch collar and necklace of seed pearls. Her hands are silk-covered wire. (Embroiderers' Guild.)

EMBROIDERED STUART PICTURES

Margaret Swain

Shire Publications Ltd

CONTENTS

Printed in Great Britain by C. I. Thomas & Sons (Haverfordwest) Ltd, Press Buildings, Merlins Bridge, Haverfordwest, Dyfed SA61 1XF.

British Library Cataloguing in Publication Data: Swain, Margaret, 1909- Embroidered Stuart Pictures. 1. Great Britain. Embroidery, history. I. Title. 746. 44'0941. ISBN 0-7478-0059-6.

ACKNOWLEDGEMENTS
My thanks are due to all the private owners and institutions who have allowed their pieces to be used as illustrations. I am especially grateful to Mary Alexander, Xanthe Brooke, Ann French, Joanna Hashagen, Santina Levey, Naomi Tarrant and Elspeth Yeo for their advice and help.

Cover: *The Rous-Lench casket, containing mirror, inkwell, glass bottles and hidden compartments. It has been preserved in an oyster-veneered olive-wood box. (Sothebys.)*

Engraving: 'David and Bathsheba', published by Gerard de Jode in 1585, from which the embroidery on page 1 derives. David stands at the top of the tower (top left), watching the attendant deliver his letter to Bathsheba. In the embroidery the letter has been omitted. (National Library of Scotland.)

2

Hannah Smith's cabinet. Her signed note tells how it was made in Oxford in 1654-6 and made up in London when she was nearly twelve. The side panels show 'Winter', an old man before a fire. The front doors portray Deborah and Barak and Jael and Sisera. 305 by 177 by 255 mm. (Whitworth Art Gallery.)

INTRODUCTION

Seventeenth-century needlework panels are to be found in country houses and museums in Britain and North America. The modern embroiderer marvels at the virtuosity of the technique, the fine silk tent stitch over one thread, the exquisite lace-stitch garments of the padded raised figures and the uninhibited use of other materials: chenille, wire, beads, sequins and mica. Even those with no interest in needlework find the pictures fascinating. The doll-like figures, wearing the opulent fashions of the Stuart court, depict the stories of the Old Testament in a landscape crowded with animals, insects, birds, fishpools, mermaids, shepherds, buildings and rainbows.

Fine tent stitch, which was often used, can reproduce a design more accurately, but the liveliness of embroidery in high relief gives the scene a theatrical impact and vitality. Raised or embossed work, as it was called (the term 'stumpwork' is a Victorian misnomer), reached its peak in the second half of the seventeenth century. It was not a new technique; it had been practised by professional embroiderers on the continent of Europe for more than a century. Indeed, a cope, now in the treasury of Aachen Cathedral, has a hood embellished with tiny three-dimensional birds worked in metal thread. It was worn at the coronation of the emperor Sigismond in 1414 and may

3

have been made even earlier. Other continental vestments show realistic figures in high relief, often decorated with seed pearls.

In England, in the reign of Elizabeth I, men's caps and women's coifs and sleeves sometimes displayed raised flower petals, insects or realistic pea-pods within the curving stems of interlaced or plaited stitches in metal thread.

The technique, therefore, was not new. However, the fashion for small needlework pictures, many of them in raised work, seems to have flowered in the reign of Charles I, flourished during the Commonwealth and the Restoration of

Above: *The lid of Hannah Smith's cabinet: 'Joseph Being Raised from the Pit' and sold to the Midianites (Genesis 37, 28). The figures of Joseph and the two men raising him are taken, in mirror image, from an engraving by Gerard de Jode. The figure on the right has a coat worked in detached lace stitches. (Whitworth Art Gallery.)*

Left: *Engraving by Gerard de Jode: 'Joseph Being Raised from the Pit' from 'Thesaurus Sacrarum Historiarum Veteris Testamenti', Antwerp, 1585. (National Library of Scotland.)*

4

Charles II and withered by the end of the seventeenth century, though one or two survive that were made in the reign of Queen Anne, the last of the Stuart dynasty, who died in 1714.

Who made them? Some bear initials. Hannah Smith, whose casket is now in the Whitworth Art Gallery, Manchester, was the only person to document the working and making up of her box, which was completed between 1654 and 1656. The names of only a handful of others are known, but they indicate that this pictorial embroidery was the culmination of a girl's training in needlework, starting with plain sewing and the sampler, progressing to lace stitches and raised and padded work with gold. This was sometimes tried out on a sampler before starting the picture or 'satin piece'. We can only marvel at the amount of time that must have been expended on these masterpieces.

Who designed them? Certainly not the workers themselves, as used to be believed. At least one designer inscribed his name and address: John Nelham, a member of the Broderers' Company of London. Other professional embroiderers must have supplied the designs and materials for so fashionable an occupation, especially during the Commonwealth, when there was no longer any demand for embroidery for the church or court. The scenes on these panels are taken from prints, woodcuts or engravings, of biblical, classical and allegorical scenes. These were not primarily intended as embroidery designs: they were often book illustrations. Such prints were used as pattern sources by silver-smiths, wood or stone carvers and tapestry designers, as well as by professional embroiderers. Amateur needlewomen could use them as well. The motifs on the fine tent-stitch panel worked in 1706 by Grisell and Rachel Baillie were all drawn directly on to the canvas from a book of engravings published in London in 1630.

Few bear dates, so that the dating of these pictures must necessarily be cautious. The fashions depicted are not always a reliable guide. The court fashion for bared breasts, seen on some of the figures in fine tent stitch, was understandably short and lasted roughly over the decade 1610 to 1620, though Queen Esther is so portrayed on a panel dated 1648 in the Burrell Collection.

Not all the pictures were framed. Boxes, mirrors, book covers, toys and sachets have all survived, though many more of these fragile confections must have perished in the intervening centuries. That so many have survived is no doubt due to family piety. The dazzling variety of techniques and the miniature scale of the work must have ensured a regard for the work of an ancestor.

The Stuart dynasty ruled the whole of Great Britain from the accession of James VI of Scotland to the English throne as James I in 1603 until the death of Queen Anne in 1714. The Puritan Commonwealth lasted from the execution of Charles I in 1649 to the Restoration of his son Charles II in 1660.

MATERIALS AND TECHNIQUE

SATIN-BASED PANELS

Thick white satin, usually with a green thread woven into the selvedge, offered a smooth rich background for the design, drawn out in ink with a fine quill pen. The drawn material was stretched on a rectangular frame for working. Smooth untwisted silk in different shades, ravelled silk like chenille (used for moss), gold thread (usually silver-gilt), metal purl (wire twisted in a spiral like a spring and often coloured), spangles (flat metal circles with a central hole, also called oes), glass beads and small pieces of mica for windows were often used to give realism to these small three-dimensional scenes. Seed pearls were often used for necklaces on the tiny figures: they sometimes formed the date or initials of the worker. On some panels silk-covered vellum strips, about 2 mm wide, are found, similar to those used by professional embroiderers to embellish the testers of beds. Many of these materials

5

A partly worked panel drawn out in ink on fine linen, with the figure of Faith with cross in the central oval. It is said to have been rescued from a house in Cheapside during the Great Fire of London in 1666. The oval is similar to that signed by John Nelham, whose premises were destroyed in the fire. (Museum of London.)

'Esther before Ahasuerus' (Esther 5, 2). Fine silk tent stitch on linen, dated in seed pearls 1648. The arms are unidentified. (Burrell Collection.)

Beadwork tray with sloping sides. The central panel shows a lady playing a lute, and a gentleman. The other details are similar to those found on embroidered panels. (Sheffield City Museum.)

must have been difficult for country needlewomen to find. It is probable that they were purchased when the drawn-out design was bought.

LINEN-BASED PANELS

Even-weave linen of a fine count provided the base for tent-stitch pictures in coloured silks, the outlines often emphasised with black silk. Worked over one thread, this gave a very precise rendering of the drawn design.

Smooth, closely woven linen was sometimes chosen rather than white satin even for raised-work pictures. This offered a satisfactory surface for the inked design and must have been easier to work on than the delicate satin. It was also used as a base for the scenes worked in *speckling*. Linen gave a firm base for beadwork panels, though elaborate trays are often found with a wire foundation only.

RAISED WORK

The stitches had already been perfected on samplers. Martha Edlin, born in 1660, worked a coloured sampler when she was eight years old, using mainly satin stitch, cross stitch and eyelet stitch. Her sampler of the following year has three rows of lace stitch meticulously worked in drawn-out squares of linen. Many similar samplers have survived from this period. She was therefore well prepared to complete her satin-covered cabinet, signed and dated 1671, when she was eleven. All the techniques required for raised work, except the actual padding, had already been learned.

Stitches included satin, flat, rococo, cross and tent stitch as well as couching. Considerable ingenuity was displayed in using these: for instance, one requiring a foundation on which the threads could be counted was worked on even-weave linen and then applied to the satin base. These flowers and plants worked on linen in rococo or tent stitch were known as *slips* and could be applied to wall hangings or

Right: Part of a long sampler signed 'Jane Turner 1668'. The female figure has a padded face and wears a lace-stitch gown with a scarf over one arm. A trial piece for a raised-work picture. (Burrell Collection.)

7

bed furnishings as well as small pictures and boxes. The lace-stitch garments and hangings were first worked, using a shape of the same size as the pattern, often with wire edges to keep the shape, before being applied to the picture. Limbs and faces were modelled over wool or tow. Sometimes carved wood was used, either covered or uncovered. Flowers, leaves and fruit were similarly stiffened with wire and padded where necessary.

The tent-stitch pictures were not confined to one stitch but could be highlighted with other stitches or even metal thread.

SPECKLING

Several larger panels survive, worked in one colour, usually a red worsted, on a plain or twilled linen. They depict numerous small scriptural scenes, outlined in reversed stem stitch ('rope stitch'), the figures shaded in fine stitches resembling dots or speckling. It is not known for what purpose these panels were made.

Above: Detail from a raised-work panel on white satin. The face and hands are painted carved wood; the gown is a fragment of silk and silver brocade; the scarf, collar, snail's shell and leaves are detached lace stitch. The fan is drawn but has not been worked.

Right: 'Speckling'. A panel worked on twilled linen in fine red worsted. The outlines are in rope stitch, the shading in fine stitches to represent dots. 'Abraham tvrning Hager and Ishmall away. Sara and Isack in ye tent. Hager in the wilderness. Eier child dieth for want of watter. The angell shoeth a well' (Genesis 21, 9-19). 995 by 175 mm. (Royal Museum of Scotland.)

Engraving: the same scene in de Jode's 'Thesaurus'.

Martha Edlin's cabinet initialled in seed pearls and worked in 1671, when she was eleven. The front panel shows Faith with book, Charity with children and Hope with an anchor. A miniature silver tea-set and candlesticks, pincushions, a bird, tiny gloves and other toys have been preserved inside. (On loan to the Victoria and Albert Museum.)

CABINETS, MIRROR FRAMES
AND BOOKBINDINGS

CABINETS

The great majority of Stuart needlework pictures have come down to us because they were mounted in a frame behind glass to be hung on a wall as evidence of their makers' expertise. The same technique and designs were used to cover boxes, mirror frames, books, pincushions and other small and precious objects. Perhaps the most endearing, because they were made up as receptacles of personal treasures, are the elaborately decorated cabinets and boxes adorned on the outside with small pictures, the silk-lined interiors often holding writing compartments with glass ink bottles, metal sand dredgers (used before blotting paper), a mirror, drawers and frequently a 'secret' drawer for rings or coins at the back. Some are furnished with pincushions, needlebooks, tape-measures or other less useful toys or conceits.

'A Cabinett', wrote Randall Holme in *The Academy of Armoury* in 1688, 'is

such as Ladys keep their rings, necklaces, Braceletts and Jewells in. It stands on the table (called the dressing table) in their Bed chamber.' The woodcut shows a cabinet with a stepped top, but they were also made with flat lids.

These remarkable examples of expertise were made by young girls as the culmination of their education as needlewomen. Hannah Smith was eleven when she made an end to her cabinet at Oxford in 1656. Martha Edlin, who had finished two meticulous samplers at the ages of eight and nine, was also eleven when she completed hers. As well as toys and a miniature silver tea-set, her cabinet contains a letter:

'This curious cabinet which came to me at the death of my mother Mrs. Martha Winter Aug. 29 1792 was the work of her grandmother Martha Edlin who was born 1660 and married Mr. Richmond . . . she had four daughters . . . the small pieces of work . . . were gifts to the worker . . .

9

The cover for a cabinet, uncut and unmounted, worked in silks on white satin. The lid, centre, shows Flora crowned with flowers, but the same portrait appears on other embroideries and is sometimes described as that of Elizabeth Coombe. Panels for the back and sides show Apollo pursuing Daphne, Pyramus and Thisbe, and Narcissus gazing at his reflection. (National Trust, Fenton House.)

also a box work'd with beads by the same person . . . and all the other work which I have of my ancestors shou'd be kept to be handed down in the Female line who may have the pleasure I now enjoy of admiring the work which has been preserved with such care for so long a time . . .'

An unmounted panel shows how these cabinets were drawn out for working. The top, sides and drawer strips were drawn close together so that none of the thick white satin was wasted. The cut edges, after being glued on to the wooden frame, were neatened with a border of

silver gimp. The top of the cabinet shows an oval panel embellished with foliage in the style of John Nelham, containing a portrait of an unknown woman who appears in other ovals of the same type. The exterior cover is complete: no strips for the front or inner drawers are included. It may have been intended to complete these in laid stitches, which would not require drawing out.

Although the majority of these cabinets are covered in white satin, one is worked with great precision on vellum or paper. Unlike the unmounted panels at Fenton House, Hampstead, with figures

Left: The lid of a cabinet, worked on vellum, not satin: laid stitches in silk. Rebecca gives the servant of Abraham a drink from the well (Genesis 24, 17-21). The design derives from an engraving by de Jode. Outside dimension 305 by 255 by 170 mm. (Burrell Collection.)

Right: The engraving 'Rebecca at the Well' from the 'Thesaurus' by de Jode.

taken from a wide variety of stories, this cabinet is restricted to scenes from the life of Isaac: 'The Sacrifice of Isaac', 'Abraham Sending His Servant for Rebecca', and 'The Meeting of Isaac and Rebecca'. On the lid Rebecca is shown at the well giving newly drawn water to Abraham's servant Elizier after his journey to find a bride for his master's son. The interior of the box, which follows the standard construction, is lined with salmon-pink silk. The top tray does not, however, hold the usual ink bottles and other fittings. Instead, it is surrounded by five segments of mirror that reflect a delicately painted scene of a boar hunt on the paper lining.

FLAT BOXES

Rectangular boxes with flat lids, larger than the cabinets with stepped tops, are often called lace boxes. Some of the interiors are padded, giving support to this theory, though it may be a modern distinction. Others have two front doors, with a lift-out tray containing inkwells or even drawers underneath. It is obvious that each box was custom-made to display the embroidery, with the interior fitted to the requirements of its owner. Like the cabinets, the flat boxes are mounted on spherical feet, often gilded. Several are dated: 1667 (Lady Lever Art Gallery); 1678, signed EC (Victoria and Albert Museum, T143.1954); 1688, signed HD for Hannah Downes (Victoria and Albert Museum, T31.1935); 1693, signed EI (private collection). The Art Institute of Chicago has a casket signed RS IP, dated 1668.

A box now in the Guildford Museum has a removable mirror inside the lid, held in place by clips. The lining is quilted blue silk. It contains a layette of fine linen (shirt trimmed with hollie point, mittens, caps and bibs) and a copy from the Cobham, Surrey, parish register of the baptism of Henry Wakeford on 10th December 1707. The family lived at Chilbrook Farm, Cobham. There is no evidence that Henry died in infancy, but his mother, Mary Wakeford, was buried on the day the infant Henry was baptised.

The cover for a box, complete but never made up, now mounted on a wooden block. The padded figures, wearing garments of detached lace stitch, depict Jepthah being greeted by his daughter (Judges 11, 30). On what were to have been the front doors, Solomon receives the Queen of Sheba. Top 205 by 270 mm. (Bowes Museum.)

A box with richly decorated lid in raised work and detached lace stitches, showing scenes from the story of Esther. The top shows Esther and Ahasuerus. The side panel shows Ahasuerus, unable to sleep, being read the acts of his reign (Esther 6, 1). The box is in prime condition because it has its own brown leather case, stamped with gold. 210 by 385 by 285 mm. (Metropolitan Museum of Art, New York.)

The box and baby clothes may have been her work.

A magnificent flat box now in the Metropolitan Museum of Art, New York, shows scenes from the story of Esther. The top depicts Esther before Ahasuerus: he is seated under a canopy with striped blue and white curtains hanging free. Esther, crowned, wearing a red striped gown and blue and white stole, is attended by two opulently dressed ladies, all with the fashionable

Left: The top of a box, in the style of John Nelham, showing a lady and a gentleman. The box is lined with quilted blue silk and contains a layette. (Guildford Museum.)

Right: Part of a layette — cap, mittens, bib and forehead cloth — found in the box, together with a copy of the entry of baptism of Henry Wakeford at Cobham, Surrey, in 1707. His mother, Mary Wakeford, was buried the same day. The box and layette may have been her work. (Guildford Museum.)

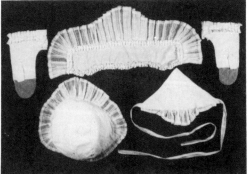

seed-pearl necklace at their throats. The interior, lined with pink silk and velvet, contains drawers and a sunken tray with small mirrors surrounding a coloured print, glass ink bottles, a double tray for pens and two sand containers. Printed on the base of the tray is: 'Sold by John Overton at the White Horse Inn'. John Overton was a printseller who stocked many of the prints used as designs for these needlework pictures. His business was situated at the sign of the White Horse in Little Britain, London, from 1667 to 1707.

Other flat boxes display miniature gardens below or on top of the lid. One (Victoria and Albert Museum, T23.1928) shows a formal garden, divided into four plots on green velvet, with fruit trees in lace stitch stiffened with wire and four ivory statues. Another has sheep under trees attended by a seated shepherdess on top of the lid. It is the charming fantasy of such conceits, as well as the dazzling expertise of the young workers, that makes these boxes so attractive.

MIRROR FRAMES

Quicksilvered glass for mirrors was a new manufacture in Britain in the seventeenth century. Because of their fragility and cost mirror plates were generally small. It is therefore not surprising that the small mirrors found inside the lids of Stuart cabinets should have been placed there to protect a precious possession.

Table or wall mirrors required frames to protect and enlarge them. Wooden or

The interior of a padded box, lined with green silk, said to have been given by Catharine of Braganza to her secretary. The mirror in the lid is held by clips and conceals a hidden compartment. (Guildford Museum.)

The exterior of the padded box. The top in fine tent stitch shows Esther and Ahasuerus. The base is covered in green velvet. 230 by 230 by 190 mm. (Guildford Museum.)

tortoiseshell frames survive. Some of the most opulent mirrors have carved wooden frames overlaid with silver, with a matching table and pair of candlestands to complete the ensemble.

Embroidered frames were also made, worked on white satin, using the same techniques and drawn out with the same figures that were chosen for pictures and boxes. A very simple rectangular frame has doors lined with stamped pink silk to protect the mirror within.

More elaborate examples survive with curved or fretted edges, the raised figures wearing garments of lace stitches. In 1649, among the possessions of the executed King Charles I was 'a large looking glass sett in a frame of needlework embroydered with the 3 faculties and the 7 Liberall sciences'. No mirror showing personifications of the Seven Liberal Arts or Sciences, (Grammar, Logic, Rhetoric, Arithmetic, Geometry, Music and Astronomy) is known, but personifications of the Virtues — Faith, with cross, Hope with anchor and, less frequently, Charity — can be found, not always together, on a mirror frame.

Above: A flat box fitted with ink bottles. The mirror, clipped into the lid, is protected by the quilted silk lining. (Phillips.)

Below: The exterior of the box. The lid shows a version of the so-called portrait of Elizabeth Coombe, said to be 'the most celebrated needlewoman of her day'. (Phillips.)

Above left: *A mirror frame with doors to protect the glass. Flat stitch and spangles on white satin. The doors are lined with stamped pink silk, the back with red velvet. The mirror can stand or be hung. 373 by 300 mm. (Royal Ontario Museum.)*

Above right: *A convex mirror frame. Raised work on white satin. The hands of the figures are carved wood, the faces padded. The costumes are worked in silk thread embellished with pearls, coral and feathers. Tortoiseshell border. 495 by 385 mm. (Burrell Collection.)*

Below: *Unmounted panels for a mirror frame. Raised work on white satin. Ovals: Paris and Pallas Athene. Circles: the Four Continents. (Lady Lever Art Gallery.)*

15

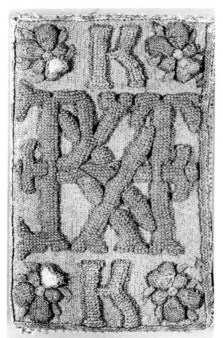

An embroidered bookbinding. 'How We Ought to Know God', a manuscript written in 1545 for Katherine Parr by the Princess Elizabeth. Red, blue and silver thread. The flowers are padded. The interlaced initials read 'Katherine Henry'. 145 by 100 mm. (Scottish Record Office.)

NEEDLEWORK BOOKBINDINGS

Many needlework covers for books survive from the first half of the seventeenth century. It was not a new fashion: it appears to have been a particularly English custom to enclose precious books or presentation copies in covers of needlework. The earliest known is a manuscript copy of the Psalms, written in the thirteenth century and given its cover in the fourteenth century. It belonged to Anne Felbrigge, a nun in the order of minoresses at Bruisyard, Suffolk, and is now in the Bodleian Library, Oxford.

Right: 'The Psalms of David', manuscript written by Esther Inglis, 1615, and dedicated to James I and VI. Cover embroidered in silver purl on red velvet. Oval medallion: a phoenix standing on a ground of green and yellow silk. 88 by 57 mm. (National Library of Scotland.)

The future Queen Elizabeth I of England made four notebooks as New Year gifts for her father, Henry VIII, and his last wife, Katherine Parr, in 1544 and 1545. One is in the Bodleian Library, one in the British Museum and one in the Scottish Record Office. The fourth has disappeared. In carefully written script, at the ages of eleven and twelve, she translated prayers composed by her stepmother into French, Italian and Latin for her father. For her stepmother, Katherine Parr, she translated from the French *The Mirror of the Sinful Soul*, and the following year the first chapter of Calvin's *Institutes*. The covers of all these small books appear to be home-made, with interlacing initials and heartsease in the corners, and strongly suggest that the young Princess Elizabeth had a hand in their making.

Other books with textile covers in velvet and silk survive, but the greatest number, many of them pictorial, appear to belong to the first half of the seventeenth century. Most of them are professional work. Small volumes of the New Testament and Psalms, sometimes *dos à dos* (the edges of one facing the spine of the other), worked in tent stitch or on

satin with raised work, can be found dated to the 1630s. A petition was submitted to Archbishop Laud in 1638 by the milliners (sellers of small wares, not confined to hats) of the Royal Exchange on behalf of the 'Imbroderers working in their own homes' who had for many years covered Bibles, Testaments and Psalm books for the nobility and gentry.

Not all were professionals, however. A small book of Psalms, 1633, 4 by 3 inches (100 by 75 mm), bound in white satin with a raised design of a vine and a rose spray, contains a note that the cover was worked by Elizabeth, wife of Matthew Wren, Bishop of Ely, who was uncle to the architect Sir Christopher Wren. The so-called 'nuns of Little Gidding' are claimed to have embroidered covers for the *Concordances* or illustrated scrapbooks of scripture made between 1630 and 1637 by the community set up by Nicholas Ferrar at Little Gidding in Cambridgeshire. Fuller, in *The Worthies of England,* recorded that 'their own needles were employed in learned and pious work to binde Bibles'. This is scarcely conclusive, since no embroidered copies survive and the pages of bound books always require stitching before the covers are put on.

Esther Inglis (Langlois), the calligraphist (1571-1624), is said also to have been a noted needlewoman who embroidered the covers which enclose the versions of the Psalms and other devotional works that she wrote in a variety of scripts with consummate skill. She was the daughter of Nicholas Langlois, a Huguenot who fled from France in 1572 and settled in Edinburgh, where he became master of the French school at Leith. Esther was taught calligraphy by her mother, and

A Book of Common Prayer (1639) and Bible (1640) bound in one volume. The cover shows Plenty (Ceres) with a cornucopia. The reverse shows Peace with an olive branch. Silks and metal thread on white satin. 485 by 305 mm.

presentation volumes of her work were made for Queen Elizabeth I and James I. The bindings are meticulously finished, and her skill with the pen suggests that she could have been equally skilled with a needle.

Few embroidered bindings can be found after the execution of Charles I in 1649: no doubt Puritan opinion considered them too frivolous.

THE SUBJECT MATTER

BIBLICAL PICTURES

Of all the topics chosen for Stuart needlework pictures, scenes from the Old Testament appear to have been the most popular. This is not surprising, for the right of the laity to read the Bible in the vernacular was an issue bitterly fought for at the Reformation. A century later the reading of the scriptures was still regarded as a duty and a privilege. Printed Bibles abounded. In addition, illustrated volumes of Old Testament history flooded Protestant countries after the Reformation. English publishers pirated the illustrations, adding an English text. Pattern drawers, who drew out the scenes on to linen or satin for working in the appropriate technique, borrowed the

Judith, who has cut off the head of Holofernes, attended by her maid, from the Book of Judith in the Apocrypha. Fine tent stitch in silks on linen. 325 by 425 mm. (Burrell Collection.)

figures, often clothing them in contemporary fashion. Kings and queens of the Old Testament were given the faces of the Stuart monarchs, taken also from engravings.

It has been suggested that biblical heroines were chosen to inculcate the virtues of obedience and sacrifice in the

'The Death of Jezebel' (II Kings 9, 30-7). The queen is thrown from the palace window. King Jehu prepares to drive over her body, but the dogs have devoured it. The vines in the background probably represent Naboth's vineyard, seized by Jezebel and her husband, King Ahab. 573 by 573 mm. (Holburne Museum.)

young needlewoman. This does not, however, explain the frequent choice of other subjects: Joseph being sold to the Midianites (on Hannah Smith's cabinet), the expulsion of Hagar and Ishmael into the wilderness, David and his adulterous union with Bathsheba, Lot and his daughters fleeing from Sodom, or the attempted seduction of Joseph by Potiphar's wife.

New Testament subjects are comparatively rare. This may be because the pictorial representation of the mother of Christ in the Nativity, for instance, could be regarded as popish in a century dominated by Puritan thought and torn by religious wars. There are, however, 'The Adoration of the Magi' (Burrell 29/163 and the Metropolitan), 'Herod's Feast', after Rubens, 'The Raising of Lazarus' (Burrell 29/74), and 'Mary Magdalen at the Feet of Christ' (Burrell 29/79). At Stoneyhurst College in Lancashire there is a chalice veil with a representation of St Winifred of Holywell, worked by Mary Bodenham, a young Catholic, who made other ecclesiastical embroideries.

CLASSICAL PICTURES

Latin formed the basis of education until the nineteenth century in all Western countries. It was the language of scholarship and in the seventeenth century serious books were still published in Latin. The history and literature

*Be his chast docke his mastres doeth him draw
To laie with him , Ioseph willeth not consent:
Wherfore cring saied, when so fast him saw,
Ioseph it was,that with force take her ment.*

E 3

Left: *'Joseph Escaping from Potiphar's Wife' (Genesis 39, 7-15). The earliest printed Bibles depicted most scenes in the open air. This, like Judith and Holofernes, has followed the old tradition. (Burrell Collection.)*

Right: *The same scene depicted by Bernard Salomon in 'Quadrins de la Bible', Lyons, 1553, published in an English edition. Though this is not the source of the needlework picture, the incident is easily recognised, even by those who could not read the verse beneath.*

Below: *'Christ at the Tomb of Lazarus'. Fine tent stitch in silk and wool. The sky is rococo stitch. Martha and Mary stand weeping. The lady, left, shows bared breasts, a fashion lasting roughly from 1610 to 1620, and wears a 'Persian' head-dress. The initials MML on the tomb may stand for Martha, Mary and Lazarus rather than be the worker's initials. 350 by 485 mm. (Burrell Collection.)*

'Alpheus and Arethusa'. The nymph Arethusa, pursued by Alpheus, is changed into a fountain by the goddess Diana, shown with bow in the clouds. Silk and metal thread on white satin. 355 by 260 mm. (Victoria and Albert Museum.)

Insequitur flagrans Arethusam veste carentem | *Sed lassata fuga, fer opem mihi Delia, clamat:*
Alpheus, timidis passibus illa fugit . | *Clamantem fusca Delia nube tegit .*
Crispin van de Passe figurauit et excudit . | *Ovid. Metam. lib. 5.*

The engraving 'Alpheus and Arethusa' by Crispin van de Passe, published in 1602. The naked Alpheus has been clothed in the needlework picture. (Victoria and Albert Museum.)

of Greece and Rome were known to all educated men and, in translation, to their less educated sisters. Even Shakespeare's comic workmen in *A Midsummer Night's Dream* were familiar with the story of Pyramus and Thisbe from the *Metamorphoses* of Ovid. The first English opera, Purcell's *Dido and Aeneas*, was composed about 1690 for a girls' boarding school in Chelsea, from the story in the *Aeneid* by Virgil.

Illustrated volumes of classical stories, especially the *Metamorphoses*, were plentiful in the seventeenth century, published in Germany and the Netherlands, as well as France, where the *Metamorphose d'Ovide figurée* appeared in Lyons as early as 1557, illustrated by Bernard Salomon, with short verses in French to tell the story. It was used as a pattern book in the same way as the illustrated Bibles. Subjects from classical literature were not, however, as popular as biblical themes, though 'Alpheus and Arethusa', 'The Judgement of Paris', 'Europa and the Bull' and other stories are found. A grisly incident related by the Greek historian Herodotus shows Queen Tomyris exulting over the severed head of Cyrus, king of the Persians.

'Diana and Acteon'. Acteon, a hunter who surprised Diana and her nymphs while they were bathing, was turned into a stag by the goddess and killed by his own hounds. Silk embroidery on white satin. 440 by 510 mm, including frame. (Lady Lever Art Gallery.)

'Fire', one of the Four Elements, Fire, Water, Earth, Air. These decorate the sides of the box containing Henry Wakeford's layette (see page 12). (Guildford Museum.)

Ceres, the Roman goddess of agriculture, appears as Plenty with a cornucopia and often represents Earth in the Four Elements (Fire, Air, Water, Earth). The female embodiments of the Five Senses can be seen, not always together, on mirrors and cabinets. Smelling is the centrepiece of the Mellerstain

panel. The Four Continents (Australia was not included until after Captain Cook's visit in 1770) are similarly depicted.

To those who embroidered them, such characters were instantly recognisable. They appear on tapestry hangings of the period, as well as in painted decorations.

Left: 'Autumn': Bacchus with vines, from the Four Seasons decorating the corners of the mirror (see page 15). (Burrell Collection.)

Right: The goddess Ceres, with cornucopia, is often used to represent Summer (see the mirror frame on page 15) in the Four Seasons or, as here, Abundance or Plenty. Each motif on this panel has been worked on fine linen in tent stitch or rococo stitch as 'slips' and then mounted on white satin. 400 by 455 mm. (Royal Museum of Scotland.)

Below: 'The Defeat of the Armada and the Gunpowder Plot'. This is one of two known panels taken from a political print published in Amsterdam in 1621. Inscribed 'To God in memory of his double deliverance from the invincible navie and the unmatcheable powder treason'. Top left: 'I blow and scatter' and 'Tilbry campe'. Above the plotters: 'In perpetual infamie of papists'. A shaft from Heaven points to 'Faux' and 'How nye 1605' and is labelled 'I see and smile'. Fine tent stitch on linen. 330 by 465 mm. (Lady Lever Art Gallery.)

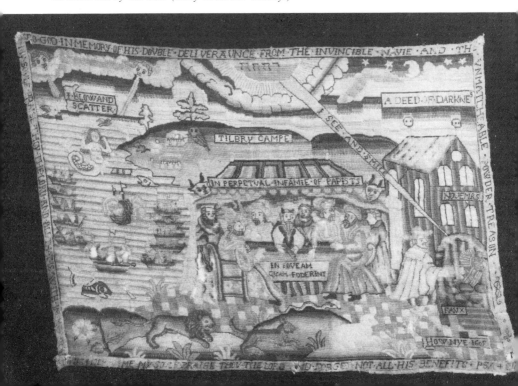

CONTEMPORARY HISTORY

The stormy history of the seventeenth century, in Britain and in Europe, where the Thirty Years War devastated cities and countryside, is scarcely reflected in the needlework pictures of the century, their scenes set for the most part in peaceful flowery landscapes.

Two similar pictures are known, based on the same political print, first published in Amsterdam in 1621. One is in the Lady Lever Art Gallery; the other is reputed to have been worked by Dame Dorothy Selby (1572-1641), whose memorial stone in Ightham church, Kent, is incised with the same scene of the defeat of the Armada, the Pope in conclave with the Devil and Guy Fawkes approaching the Houses of Parliament with his lantern. Dame Dorothy's memorial describes her:

> She was a Dorcas
> Whose Curious Needle turn'd th' abused
>   Stage
> Of this Leud World into the
>   Golden Age
> Whose Pen of Steele and Silken Inke
>   enrolled
> The Acts of Jonah in records of Gold ...
> In heart a Lydia and in tongue a
>   Hanna,
> In Zeale a Ruth, in Wedlock a
>   Susanna:
> Prudently simple, providently wary
> To th' World a Martha and to Heaven a
>   Mary.

The memorial to Dame Dorothy Selby (1572-1641), a notable needlewoman, in Ightham church, Kent. The design of 'The Defeat of the Armada and the Gunpowder Plot', which she worked, similar to the one illustrated opposite, is incised on the panel behind her.

Dame Dorothy made several other needlework pictures, including 'A Session of Parliament in the Presence of King James I'.

A raised-work picture on white satin, showing (left) Charles II in elaborately worked royal robes with his queen, Catharine of Braganza, and (right) probably his brother, the Duke of York, with Mary of Modena, his second wife. Also shown are Charles hiding in the Boscobel oak after the battle of Worcester in 1651 and his escape on horseback disguised as the servant of Jane Lane. 317 by 396 mm. (Holburne Museum.)

Queen Henrietta Maria (1606-69). Silks and purl, with seed pearls, in raised and surface stitches on white satin. The oval is in the style of John Nelham. The face is modelled and covered with silk. (Fitzwilliam Museum.)

Detail of a panel on white satin showing James I and his wife, Anne of Denmark, after his accession to the throne of Great Britain in 1603, with (below) King James and his mother, Mary, Queen of Scots. (Jedburgh Museum.)

A picture of Charles I at prayer, worked on satin with raised details, in the Victoria and Albert Museum (T117.1936) is taken from the frontispiece to a book, *Eikon Basilike, The True Pourtraieture of His Sacred Majestie in his Solitudes and Sufferings* (1648). It shows the king, kneeling, holding a crown of thorns in his hand, spurning the royal crown that lies at his feet, his eyes set on a heavenly crown. The embroidered panel adds the figure of a youthful Charles II on the left, with two angels holding a crown over his head.

Many miniature portraits of Charles I survive, some of them probably made after 1700, but almost all derive from paintings by Van Dyck and the many engravings made after them. One, however, in Judge Untermyer's collection, shows the king defiantly wearing a hat, as was his prerogative at his trial. This is copied from an engraving after a painting by Edward Bower, done in 1649 during the king's trial.

A charming portrait of Henrietta Maria is in the Fitzwilliam Museum. The moulded head is covered with silk and is enclosed in an oval frame typical of John Nelham's designs.

Portraits of Queen Anne, the last of the Stuart monarchs, based on a painting by Kneller, usually show her standing on a black and white chequered floor. Curiously, her father, James II, who went into exile in 1688, does not appear to have inspired Jacobite needlewomen to reproduce his portrait in stitchery.

24

SOURCES OF THE DESIGNS

The Stuart needlewoman did not create her own designs. The figures, biblical, classical or historical, the flowers and birds, the animals and insects were all copied from woodcuts or engravings and drawn out on to the material for the worker to embroider. The pictures showed her expertise in embroidery: they were not intended to show her skill as an artist. The same engravings were used as source material for other craftsmen: for gold and metal work, ceramics, stained glass. Even tapestries, paintings and sculptures have been found that owe their designs to an engraving. The idea that a needlewoman should make her own designs is comparatively modern and was not seriously considered before the end of the nineteenth century, except by such people as Mrs Delany, whose artistic talents included embroidery.

Prints and engravings were widely available for pattern drawers and others. Printsellers like the Overtons, father, son and grandson, who flourished from 1629 to 1707, Robert Walton in St Paul's Churchyard and Peter Stent at the White Horse in Giltspur Street may all have offered the service of drawing out designs on to fabric for working. Peter Stent's trade card of 1662 in the Bodleian Library lists over five hundred titles, including many that are found on needlework pictures:

A book of Flora, 13 plates
A book of Flowers, Beasts, Birds and

Fruits in three parts, 20 leaves in each part
A new Book of Flowers, Beasts, Birds, invented and drawn wholly by J. Dunstall
A book of Branches, slips, Flies etc. 8 Plates
The Four Seasons of the Year G. Glover sculpt.
The Five Senses, Marmion Inventer
The Five Senses, Glover sculpt
The Four Quarters of the World
The Four Complexions, in habit of 4 Nations
The Four Elements, Fire, Aire, Earth and Water . . .
Pictures lately printed in Sheets
Queen Elizabeth
King James and Queen Anne
King Charles the First and Queen Mary

Above: '*Abraham and the Angels*' (Genesis 18, 1-18). Fine tent stitch on linen with pictorial border on a dark blue ground. This was an extremely popular subject; there are many versions, most of them deriving from the engraving by de Jode. The figure with the child in the tent may represent Hagar with Ishmael. The hunter, fishpond and rural background have been added by the pattern drawer.

Left: *The engraving 'Abraham Entertaining the Angels', with Sarah listening. De Jode, 'Thesaurus Sacrarum Historiarum Veteris Testamenti', 1585.*

The Mellerstain panel. Fine tent stitch in coloured wools and silk on linen, signed 'GB', 'RB' and 'MM' and dated 1706. The initials are those of Grisell Baillie, born 1692, Rachel, her sister, born 1696, and May Menzies, their governess. All the motifs are taken from 'A Booke of Beast', published in London in 1630. The centrepiece represents 'Smelling' from the Five Senses. 330 by 495 mm. (The Earl of Haddington.)

> King Charles the Second and Queen Katherine
> Two other sorts of the King
> Duke of York, Duke of Gloucester, Prince of Orange and Princess Royal . . .

Stent's list covers most of the design elements of the pictures. Scriptural scenes derive from such illustrated Bibles as those of Jost Amman (1539-91) and *Quadrins de la Bible* (1553), published in Lyon and illustrated by Bernard Salomon, which appeared in English, German, Spanish and Italian editions. But by far the most popular appears to have been the *Thesaurus* of Old Testament history published in Antwerp in 1585 by Gerard de Jode, mainly after drawings by Martin de Vos (1531-1603). Nancy Graves Cabot identified 42 embroideries in Britain and North America from this book.

John Nelham, a member of the Broderers' Company, and his father, Roger Nelham, each left a collection of 'prints' when they died. Roger left to his son John in his will, dated 1653, 'the halfe of

The engraving 'Smelling', one of a set of the Five Senses printed by Thomas Jenner and bound into the Mellerstain copy of Thomas Johnson's book of engravings.

26

A page from 'A Booke of Beast, Birds, Flowers, Fruits, Flies, and Wormes, Exactly Drawne with Their Lively Colours Truly Described', published by Thomas Johnson in London, 1630. The peacock, fox and porcupine appear at the top of the Mellerstain panel. The marigold and olives were also copied. Note that these are taller than the peacock.

my books and prints and patterns which I do use for the drawing of workes . . . All my beames and lathes and working instruments which do appertain and belong to my worke house.' The prints were as necessary as the embroidery frames for the carrying on of a professional embroiderer's business.

When drawn-out designs could not easily be obtained, as in Scotland, these same prints were still used as patterns. In 1706 the two daughters of Lady Grisell Baillie, Rachel and Grisell, aged twelve and fourteen, worked together on a fine tent-stitch panel. Their governess, May Menzies, had a book that had belonged to her grandmother — *A Booke of Beast, Birds, Flowers, Fruits, Flies, and Wormes, Exactly Drawne . . .*, published by Thomas Johnson in London in 1630. The designs are all borrowed from earlier publications, the animals mostly from engravings by Adrian Collaert published in Antwerp around 1590; some of the flowers are from the *Hortus Floridus* (1614) of Crispin van de Passe, published in Arnhem. The drawings are crowded on to a page irrespective of scale.

When May Menzies drew out the motifs on to the canvas, she traced them exactly from the book. Thus the rose is larger than the swan, the lily larger than the rhinoceros. This helps to explain the lack of scale of the components of so many of the needlework pictures of the seventeenth century.

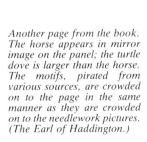

Another page from the book. The horse appears in mirror image on the panel; the turtle dove is larger than the horse. The motifs, pirated from various sources, are crowded on to the page in the same manner as they are crowded on to the needlework pictures. (The Earl of Haddington.)

27

'The Drowning of the Egyptians in the Red Sea' (Exodus 14, 23-8). Raised work on white satin. Moses stands left, his hand raised. The Israelites, safely across with their goods, stand on dry land, while Pharaoh and his army are drowned. Worked by Damaris Pearce, who died in 1679 aged twenty. (Lady Lever Art Gallery.)

THE MAKERS

The names of those who worked these pictures, like those who drew them out, are scarcely known. Hannah Smith's forthright note, written 'for those that shall inquire about it', is exceptional. Martha Edlin's descendants have told us a little more about her. We know that the year after Grisell and Rachel Baillie finished the tent-stitch panel their mother paid for white satin, silks and 'threed to the tent [frame]' for a satin piece which has not survived. Rachel's descendants still cherish the panel and book at Mellerstain.

Damaris Pearse, the daughter of a nonconformist minister, worked the wonderfully vivid 'Drowning of the Egyptians in the Red Sea'. A copy of the oration at her funeral records that she was born at Dunsford, Devon, in 1659 and lived in the village of Ermington in the same county until her death in 1679 after an illness of nearly four years. She is said to have made pieces for sale.

Dame Dorothy Selby apparently continued to embroider until her death in 1641 at the age of 69. She left an unfinished panel in fine linen, 'The Judgement of Solomon', though this may have been laid aside for some years. Others are merely names: Elizabeth Coombe, said to be 'the foremost needlewoman of her day'; Sarah Gurnall, who made a beadwork box; and Mary Slack, who inscribed her panel of Abraham and Hagar 'Doncaster 77 Mary Slack her work and by desire of Phillis Ives to be hers at my decease'.

John Nelham, whose name and address are on a satin picture at Blair Castle, and his father, Roger, are both known to have been professional embroiderers, who supplied materials as well as designs drawn out. No doubt other members of the Broderers' Company undertook similar commissions, especially under the Commonwealth, and would work pieces as samples.

An engraving, 'The Drowning of the Egyptians in the Red Sea', from de Jode's 'Thesaurus' of Old Testament history. The figures of Pharaoh and his horses on the panel opposite derive from this print. (National Library of Scotland.)

Below: *A panel on white satin worked in silks and metal thread, showing a lady and gentleman with tents enclosed in a scrolled oval. Inscribed in ink along the base is 'Jno Nelham, Suger Lofe, Greyfriars, Newgate Market'. This address was burned down in the Great Fire of London, 1666. John Nelham, a member of the Broderers' Company, moved to the Old Bailey but used the same sign. He died in 1684. 510 by 560 mm. (The Duke of Atholl, Blair Castle.)*

A panel on white satin. In the centre is Charity, with Hope on the left with an anchor and Faith on the right with a cross. The scrolled oval, the lion and the general arrangement are in the style of John Nelham. (Historic Deerfield, Massachusetts.)

Below left: 'The Visitation' of the Virgin to her cousin Elizabeth (Luke 1, 39-45). Silk and gilt thread on linen, split and couching stitches. Inscribed on the back: 'Edmund Harrison Imbroiderer to King Charles m[ade this] 1637'. One of a set depicting the life of the Virgin. 610 by 590 mm. (Royal Museum of Scotland.)

Below right: A large wall panel, 'The Finding of Moses' (Exodus 6, 5-10), bearing the initials of Baillie George Aedie and his wife, Mary Jamesone. They were married in 1677 and she died in 1684. Linen ground entirely covered by wool embroidery with silk for the flesh and some details. Four other panels of Old Testament subjects were sold to the St Nicholas Kirk, Aberdeen, in 1686 and have remained there ever since. 1520 by 2310 mm. (St Nicholas Kirk, Aberdeen.)

Edmund Harrison, embroiderer to Charles I, is now remembered for a private commission he undertook for a Catholic family: scenes from the life of the Virgin. The names of others are known: Mr Rutlish, embroiderer to Charles II, made sufficient money to endow a school that still continues at Merton, south-west London, when he died in 1687. With his partner, George Pinckney, he undertook embroidery for the king and queen, on Garter robes and liveries. Even the royal rat-killer had a coat embroidered with gold and silver purl 'with letters and crowned Rats and Wheatsheaves'.

Four needlework pictures, much larger than those pictured here, hang in St Nicholas Kirk, Aberdeen. Intended as domestic wall hangings, they are attributed to Mary Jamesone, whose initials and those of her third husband, Baillie George Aedie, appear on 'The Finding of Moses'. After her death in 1684 they were bought by the church. They are all Old Testament subjects and belong to the same tradition as the smaller Stuart needlework pictures.

FURTHER READING

Brett, K. B. *English Embroidery*. Royal Ontario Museum, Toronto, 1972.
Clabburn, Pamela. *The Needleworker's Dictionary*. Macmillan, 1976.
Davenport, C. *English Embroidered Bookbindings*. Kegan Paul, 1899.
Hackenbroch, Y. *English and Other Needlework . . . in the Irwin Untermyer Collection*. Thames and Hudson, 1960.
Nevinson, J. L. *Catalogue of English Domestic Embroidery*. Victoria and Albert Museum, 1938 and 1950.
Seligman, G. S., and Hughes, T. *Domestic Needlework*. Country Life, 1926.
Swain, M. *Historical Needlework*. Barrie and Jenkins, 1970.
Swain, M. *Figures on Fabric*. A. and C. Black, 1980.
Symonds, M., and Preece, L. *Needlework through the Ages*. Hodder and Stoughton, 1928.
Synge, L. (editor). *The Royal School of Needlework Book of Needlework and Embroidery*. Collins, 1986.

PLACES TO VISIT

Many museums or country houses display embroidered Stuart pictures or cabinets. The following have notable collections, though it is always advisable to write in advance, as the pieces may not be on display.

GREAT BRITAIN
Ashmolean Museum of Art and Archaeology, Beaumont Street, Oxford OX1 2PH. Telephone: 0865 278000.
Blair Castle and Atholl Museum, Blair Atholl, Pitlochry, Perthshire PH18 5TL. Telephone: 079681 207.
The Bowes Museum, Barnard Castle, County Durham DL12 8NP. Telephone: 0833 690606.
The Burrell Collection, Pollock Country Park, 2060 Pollockshaws Road, Glasgow G43 1AT. Telephone: 041-649 7151.
Fenton House, Windmill Lane, Hampstead, London NW3 6RT. Telephone: 01-435 3471.
Fitzwilliam Museum, Trumpington Street, Cambridge CB2 1RB. Telephone: 0223 332900.

Guildford Museum, Castle Arch, Quarry Street, Guildford, Surrey GU1 3SX. Telephone: 0483 444751.
Holburne Museum and Crafts Study Centre, Great Pulteney Street, Bath, Avon BA2 4DB. Telephone: 0225 66669.
Kellie Castle, by Pittenweem, Anstruther, Fife KY10 2RF. Telephone: 03338 271.
Lady Lever Art Gallery, Port Sunlight Village, Wirral, Merseyside L62 5EQ. Telephone: 051-645 3623.
Royal Museum of Scotland, Chambers Street, Edinburgh EH1 1JF. Telephone: 031-225 7534.
Victoria and Albert Museum, Cromwell Road, South Kensington, London SW7 2RL. Telephone: 01-938 8500.
Whitworth Art Gallery, University of Manchester, Oxford Road, Manchester M15 6ER. Telephone: 061-273 4865.

CANADA
Royal Ontario Museum, 100 Queen's Park, Toronto, Ontario M5C 2C6.

UNITED STATES OF AMERICA
Art Institute of Chicago, Michigan Avenue at Adams Street, Chicago, Illinois 60603.
Historic Deerfield, The Street, Deerfield, Massachusetts 01342.
Metropolitan Museum of Art, 5th Avenue at 82nd Street, New York, NY 10028.
The St Louis Art Museum, Forest Park, St Louis, Missouri 63110.